The story of sea otters

by William Weber Johnson

illustrated with photographs, prints, and map

Random House 🏠 New York

For their help in the preparation of this book, the author would like to thank: William F. Bryan, Salinas, California; Dr. Raymond Gilmore, San Diego Natural History Museum, San Diego, California; Captain Russell Goodrich, California Department of Fish & Game, Santa Barbara, California; William Harwood, Morro Bay, California; Dr. Karl Kenyon, Fish and Wildlife Service, U.S. Department of the Interior, Seattle, Washington; Dr. George Lindsay, California Academy of Sciences, San Francisco, California; Dr. James Mattison, Jr., Salinas, California; Dr. Wheeler North, California Institute of Technology, Pasadena, California; Mrs. Margaret Owings, Friends of the Sea Otter, Big Sur, California; Dr. Robert Orr, California Academy of Sciences, San Francisco, California; Ernest Porter, Atascadero, California; Judson Vandevere, Monterey, California.

The publisher is grateful to Dr. Karl Kenyon, Fish and Wildlife Service, U.S. Department of the Interior, Seattle, Washington, for his generous assistance in the preparation of this book.

Library of Congress Cataloging in Publication Data

Johnson, William Weber, 1909– The story of sea otters.
SUMMARY: A history of the sea otter which discusses their habits and ecological decline. I. Title. 1. Sea-otters—Juvenile literature. [1. Sea otters] I. Title.
QL737.C25J63   599′.74447   72-11057
ISBN 0-394-82403-2   ISBN 0-394-92403-7 (lib. bdg.)

For
Gregory and Rebecca Jones
Mary Hunter
Anne and Elizabeth Ellegood

Contents

PICTURE CREDITS: Ann Bryan, 73; William F. Bryan, cover, front endpaper; Ron Church (Photography Unlimited), facing title page, 8, 14, 16, 17, 20, 22, 24-25, 35, 79, 82; from Captain James Cook, *Voyage to the Pacific, Atlas to the Second Edition, 1785* (courtesy New York Public Library, Rare Book Room), 57; Edward S. Curtis (courtesy Pacific Search Books), 60; Tom Hollyman (Photo Researchers), 70; courtesy Kelco Company, 81; Karl W. Kenyon, 3, 27 (Bureau of Sport Fisheries and Wildlife), 28, 33, 45 (National Audubon Society); James A. Mattison, Jr., M.D., 11, 19, 87; John Mattison, 23; Richard Mattison, 84; Steve McCutcheon (Alaska Pictorial Service), 5, 36, 40, 54, 75; William Morgan (courtesy James A. Mattison, Jr., M.D.), 52; New York Public Library, Picture Collection, 47; Ed Park, 32; *Scientific American* (May, 1906), 42; from H. J. Snow, *In Forbidden Seas: Recollections of Sea Otter Hunting in the Kurils, 1910* (courtesy New York Public Library), 50, 64 (both), 65 (both), 66 (photo by Clara L. Minard); from George Vancouver's journal (courtesy New York Public Library), 59. Map by Charlotte Staub.

The story of sea otters

1
The lost pup

One gray and stormy day several years ago, a strong west wind whipped up heavy surf along the rocky shore of Carmel Bay on the coast of California. Huge waves from far out in the Pacific thundered in on the rocks and sent sheets of water high in the air.

A man who lived near the shore heard cries in the storm. He thought at first that they came from an injured sea bird. But then he saw a tiny, furry creature tossing helplessly about in the surf. Crying pitifully, it sank under the force of a giant wave, then rose and cried again. It was headed straight for the dangerous rocks.

The man rushed across the beach and waded into the water between the boulders. The ocean current sucked sand out from under his feet, but he managed to make his way by holding on to the rocks. Finally he was able to reach out and grab the animal by its hind legs.

He was just in time. A moment later and the creature would have been crushed on the rocks—or drowned. When the man pulled it from the waves, salt water poured from its mouth.

The animal was a baby sea otter, only a few weeks old. The otter pup's home was the big bed of giant kelp—a kind of seaweed—a few hundred yards offshore. The mother otter had probably left the pup in the kelp bed while she went in search of food for both of them. The heavy seas had washed the pup out of the kelp.

The rescuer rubbed the pup dry with towels and fed it warm milk from a nursing bottle. Then he telephoned a marine biologist, who came with his 12-year-old son to see the little otter.

Later that day they took the pup back to the water's edge, put it down, and waited. A grown otter appeared beyond the surf—probably the pup's mother. Raising herself in the water, she looked toward the shore and made the same sad cry the pup had made, but in a deeper tone. She did not come closer. The surf was too heavy for even a big otter to swim through safely.

The men and the boy spent the night on the beach

with the pup to make sure no harm came to it. During the night the pup snuggled in the boy's sleeping bag and slept soundly.

In the morning the surf was still high. Two divers offered to take the pup back out to the kelp bed. They fastened a wire basket to a surfboard, put the young otter in the basket, and swam out with the board. They carefully placed the pup in the kelp, draping strands of the seaweed around it so that it could not float away again. Then they backed away and watched.

The otter pup was crying again. A big otter swam up, rose out of the water, and listened to the cries. She went to the pup and clutched it to her body with her forelegs. Then, lying on her back with the pup on her chest, she swam away to another part of the kelp where there were several dozen other otters. The pup stopped crying.

Several people—the rescuer, the biologist and his son, and the divers—had gone to a lot of trouble for the sake of one small animal. But this part of the world—the central California coast—is one of the few places where the sea otter still lives. People here regard the otters with affection and admiration—and wonder, too. Sea otters have had a troubled history, and it is almost a miracle that they can still be seen and enjoyed as they play in their kelp-bed homes.

2
The kelp dwellers

The giant beds of kelp along the Pacific coast are like forest thickets. The strong stems of this greenish-brown seaweed are fastened securely to the ocean bottom. The plants rise to the surface, 100 feet or more, like slender, many-branched trees growing together. The tides and currents sway them back and forth, just as the wind sways forest trees. At the surface the kelp plants spread out in a great canopy, like treetops. The stems and leaves of the kelp are kept afloat by air-filled bulbs that grow on the stems.

Just as the forest is home for many birds and animals, the kelp shelters many sea creatures. Crabs and snails live on the stems and among the leaves. On the ocean bottom, where the kelp is fastened to rocks, are sea urchins, mussels, clams, starfish, and big sea

snails called abalone. Fish, both small and large, swim in and out of the underwater thickets.

But the largest and most appealing of the kelp dwellers is the sea otter.

The otter, with legs and ears and a thick fur coat, looks more like a land animal than a sea creature. Its wide-set eyes are black and shiny. The coat is brownish-black—and glistening black when the otter is wet all over—but there are long white whiskers and much white hair around the face and head. For this reason some people have called the otter the "old man of the sea."

Other people have called sea otters the "clowns of the kelp beds." The animals tumble about as clowns do in a circus ring. Their fur coats look many sizes too large for them, like baggy suits. And, just as clowns sometimes wear oversize shoes on the wrong feet, the otter has large hind feet that seem to be reversed. The big toes are on the outside of the feet and the little toes are on the inside.

These large hind feet are flattened, and they act like flippers. Because of them, the sea otter is a strong, graceful swimmer and an expert underwater hunter. By pumping its hind feet up and down, the otter can dive 150 feet or more below the surface to hunt for food or to escape from danger. Most of the dives last

An underwater kelp "forest." The kelp plants are held upright by the air-filled bulbs on the stems.

A sea otter at rest in a kelp bed.

for a minute or a minute and a half, but the otter can
stay down for four minutes or more, covering a large
area of the ocean bottom.

The sea otters spend their lives in and around the
kelp beds and seldom go ashore. They find their food
in and under the kelp. Sometimes they eat the crabs
and snails that live near the surface. Sometimes they
dive for small squid (relatives of the octopus) and
small, slow-moving fish. These they catch with the
claws of their front feet—retractable claws that, like a
cat's, can be pulled back into the toes when not
needed.

But the otter's favorite food is shellfish from the
ocean floor. Some kinds of shellfish, such as sea ur-

16

chins and mussels, are easily gathered and the otter can pick up a number of them on a single dive. Others are anchored securely to the rocks. To get these, the otter does something that is very unusual in the animal world: it selects and uses a tool. It picks up a stone from the bottom, holds the stone in both forepaws, and hammers the shellfish loose from the rock.

If the otter is trying to get an abalone, which has a thick, hard shell and which clings very tightly to the rock, the otter may run out of breath before it can

Using a large stone, a sea otter hammers an abalone loose from a rock on the ocean floor. The claws of the otter's front feet are extended in this picture.

loosen the shell. In this case the otter will return to the surface, take a breath, and dive again. It may have to dive a dozen or more times before it can free the abalone.

All the shellfish the otter collects are tucked into loose folds of skin under the forelegs. So is the stone, as soon as the otter has finished hammering with it.

After surfacing with the shellfish, the otter breathes deeply and looks around. Then it turns on its back and floats in a relaxed position. The forepaws are held together on the chest. The flipper-like hind feet and the flattened tail extend out of the water, pointing back toward the otter's head.

Having rested, the otter pulls the stone out from under a foreleg and places the tool on its chest. Now the stone will be put to a new use. One by one, the otter brings out the shellfish from under its other foreleg. Seizing them with both forepaws, it beats them on the stone to break the shells and expose the meat. Finally the otter eats, chuckling and slurping with enjoyment.

The sea otter is a hearty eater. A full-grown otter weighs about 70 or 80 pounds—about the same as a husky 10-year-old child. But the otter eats much more than a child, or even an adult human being. In a single day, a human being may eat 3 or 4 pounds of

A sea otter smashes a mussel open against the stone on its chest.

food, while an otter may eat 15 or 20 pounds—one-fourth of its own body weight. Only by eating a lot can the sea otter get the energy and body heat needed for its life in cold water.

When the feast is finished, the otter rolls over and over in the water to get rid of the shells, scraps, and fishy slime—and usually the stone tool, too. Often gulls sit on the water nearby, waiting for the otter to roll. Then they snatch at whatever scraps are left. The otter pays no attention to them.

While the otter eats a sea urchin, the sea gull waits for leftovers.

After several rolls, the otter once again floats on its back. Now it scratches its head with a forepaw, as though puzzled. Actually, the otter is cleaning its fur, using the retractable claws as a comb and the forepaws as brushes. The otter squeezes out water and fluffs up its fur on all parts of the body above the water line.

The sea otter is one of the cleanest of all animals—for good reason.

Unlike other animals that live in the ocean—such as whales, seals, and walruses—the otter has no layer of fat or blubber to protect it from the cold of the sea. Its only protection is its thick fur coat. The fur holds a layer of warm air between the otter's body and the water. This air also makes it possible for the otter to float easily—and much of its life is spent floating.

If the otter's fur became soiled with food, oil, or dirt of any kind, it could no longer hold the air. The otter would be unable to float and would have to swim all the time, day and night, which it could not do. Worse, it would soon become too chilled to live. Instinctively, the otter avoids this fate by spending much of its time grooming and cleaning its fur.

After a meal, the otter may go to sleep, floating on its back with its head up. Or it may join other otters in play. The animals roll over, turn somersaults, make short dives, and chase each other. Sometimes they leave the kelp bed and swim toward the shore to ride the waves and tumble about in the surf.

When a boat comes near, the otters raise themselves in the water and stare. They can raise about one-third of their bodies above the surface. They make signs of alarm with their forepaws, extending them with palms out or clutching them to their faces. Although

Sea otters at play.

A sea otter raises its forepaws in alarm while floating on its back. The strands of kelp lying across its stomach keep the otter from drifting away while sleeping.

they are not as timid as many wild animals, they do not like human beings to come too close.

If people do come near, the otters leave. Some swim away by lying on their backs and paddling rapidly with their hind feet. Others make a series of leaps out of the water, like porpoises, to get away quickly. But a few continue to stare, allowing the boat to come quite near before they dive and disappear.

A raft of sea otters in a kelp bed off the California coast.

3
Mothers and pups

Sea otters tend to stay together in the kelp beds, sometimes in groups of a dozen or so, sometimes in crowds of a hundred or more. Such groups are called "rafts." Usually one raft will be made up of male otters, another of females and pups.

Some of the females have raw, red noses. This is a sign that they have recently mated, because the male otter often bites the female on the nose while mating.

Among sea otters, a male and female do not stay together long. A male seeks out a female and spends up to three days eating, sleeping, and mating with her. Then the female leaves him—sometimes by sneaking away—and he finally returns to his raft.

Mating can take place at any time during the year. As a result, pups of different ages are found in the mother-and-pup raft. No one knows for sure whether the pups are born on land or in the water. The mother otter bears only one pup at a time. In the ocean it would be difficult, if not impossible, for her to take care of more than one.

People who live along the California coast spend hours looking through binoculars at the mother otters with their pups. Other people travel long distances in the hope of seeing them, for they are among the most touching sights in nature. Few baby animals receive as much loving attention from their mothers.

Much of the time the mother otter floats on her back, cradling the little otter with her forelegs. At first, the pup looks like a seagoing teddy bear. When it is very young, its fur is tawny-colored, much lighter than that of the parents. The mother hugs the pup,

A mother sea otter cradles her pup.

licks it with her tongue, and fluffs up its fur again and
again, keeping its coat as clean as her own.

When the pup is hungry, the mother otter lifts it in
the air, turns it around, and puts it down so that it can
nurse. The pup gets a supply of rich milk from the
two nipples on the mother's lower belly.

Later, when it can eat solid food, the mother places
the pup among the strands of kelp to keep it from
drifting away. Then she dives to bring up fish or shell-

fish for both of them. While the mother is away, the young otter often cries, just as a human baby does when it is hungry and alone.

Sometimes the mother and pup are disturbed by the approach of a human being or some other possible danger. The mother may tuck the young otter under one foreleg and dive out of sight. Or, if the pup is too large to fit under her foreleg, she may seize its loose-fitting fur in her teeth and pull it underwater with her.

A pup floats beside its mother while she grooms her fur.

Pups occasionally drown during these escape dives.

The pup depends upon the mother for the first year of its life. By the time it is a year old, it may be as large as its mother. Now the pup is usually impatient for food. Instead of waiting for the mother to give it food, the pup may try to take it away from her, and the two appear to be fighting fiercely.

Much of the time the mother otter and her pup play together in the water, swimming and making short dives. The pup knows how to swim a little at birth. But it needs many practice sessions to become an expert swimmer and diver—which it must become if it is to survive in the ocean. Diving is more difficult for the pup than swimming because the air trapped in its fur tends to keep it on the surface. The pup must learn how to drive itself down through the water with a strong up-and-down motion of its hind feet and tail.

When the pup does manage to reach the bottom, it may at first bring up useless things—pebbles, scraps of seaweed, or anything else that catches its eye. But by watching its mother and eating the things she brings to the surface, it learns what is good and useful and what is not. And it learns, in time, to use rocks as tools, just as the adult otters do. The young otter soon becomes perfectly suited to life in the ocean.

4
The animals
that went to sea

Once upon a time the sea otters lived on land. But about a million years ago they left the land and went to live in the sea. They have lived there ever since.

Other animals did this, too—the whales, porpoises, dolphins, seals, sea lions, elephant seals, and walruses. So did the huge cowlike animals known as manatees and dugongs. All were land animals once. No one knows why they moved to the sea.

All of these animals were mammals. That is, they bore their young alive and nursed them. They were warm-blooded, keeping the same body temperature in all weathers. And they breathed oxygen from the air.

Even though these animals now spend most of their lives in the water, they are still mammals—not fish. A fish takes oxygen from the water instead of the air.

The temperature of a fish changes with the temperature of the water. And most fish lay eggs.

In time, some of the mammals that deserted the land—the whales, porpoises, and dolphins, for example—came to look like fish, with streamlined bodies and fins. But the sea otter, the smallest of these oceanic mammals, still looks a lot like its relatives that continue to live on land. Only its hind feet and tail changed shape over the years.

All otters, both those that live on land and those that live in the sea, belong to the mustelid family. The family includes such animals as minks, weasels, skunks, and badgers. The otters form a large group within the mustelid family. Various species, or kinds, of otters are found in all parts of the world except Australia, New Zealand, Madagascar, and the arctic and antarctic regions.

North American otters, often called river otters, are the kind usually seen in zoos. They are about three to four feet long and weigh from 10 to 30 pounds. River otters are excellent swimmers and catch much of their food in the water. Sometimes they even swim out to sea. But they are still land animals. They make their homes on land and they bear their young there. River otters are often kept in captivity and some people have even made household pets of them. There are stories

*Above: A river otter, with its long, tapered tail.
Right: A sea otter has a blunter tail and larger hind
feet. This sea otter is holding squid in the loose
skin under its foreleg.*

of river otters that have been tamed and taught to catch fish for their owner's table.

The sea otter is different from the river otter in many ways. It is longer—as much as five feet long—and much heavier. It is the largest of all otters. Because of its flipper-like hind feet, the sea otter has difficulty in walking or running when it comes ashore, which it seldom does. Its tail, instead of being tapered like the river otter's, is blunter and flattened. The sea otter moves its tail up and down while swimming,

getting an extra push, while the river otter merely uses its long tail as a rudder. On the surface of the water, the sea otter almost always swims on its back; the river otter usually swims belly-down. Although the sea otter gives birth to one pup at a time, the river otter bears three or four at once. It is easier for a mother otter to care for pups on land.

Like river otters, sea otters can become friendly with people. Ocean divers have found that otters can be approached easily underwater and that they gladly accept gifts of food. At times, sea otters can be fed by hand from a boat—but they do not like to be touched. In captivity they learn to recognize people who feed them.

All otters and most other mustelids have fine, thick fur. For many centuries, natives of North America and Siberia used these animals' skins for clothing because they gave good protection against the cold. But because the skins were beautiful and rare, they became symbols of power and wealth, as did many other fine furs. The skins of ermines and sables—both weasel-like animals—were badges of royalty in many parts of Europe and Asia. The skins of beavers (nonmustelids) were once used as money in North America, first by the Indians and later by the white men.

The rich sea otter skins were to become the most

valuable of all pelts. But until the 18th century very few people knew about them. The Indians and Eskimos of the northwest coast of North America had hunted sea otters for many years, and so had the Aleuts who lived on the chain of islands that stretch for 900 miles from Alaska to Siberia. These people had little

A sea otter accepts a squid from a diver.

The sea otter has the most luxurious fur of any animal.

interest in the sea otter's flesh. They preferred fish, seal, and whale meat. Mainly they wanted the otter's loose-fitting fur coat, which they stretched and made into warm blankets, robes, and shirts. The skin from a sea otter five feet long could be stretched to six feet.

These natives respected the otter's intelligence. They thought the otter could remove an arrow or spear from its flesh by biting off the end. They also believed that the otter, when surrounded by hunters, would sometimes dive to the bottom and wedge itself in the rocks. There, they said, it would drown rather than be captured. Some people of the Kamchatka Peninsula, off the Siberian coast, even thought the otter was a branch of the human race. Otherwise how could it be so crafty and intelligent?

Although early hunters killed many sea otters, the herds were large and continued to flourish. They were found in shallow waters around the rim of the North Pacific Ocean—all the way from the northern islands of Japan, along the coast of Siberia, across to Alaska, and down the coast of North America to as far south as Baja California.

Later, when Europeans discovered these great herds of otters, they described them as a "river of fur," a river that stretched all the way from one continent to another.

5

Bears? beavers? apes?

The first European explorers to see the great "river of fur" in the North Pacific did not know what the animals were. Some called them bears. Some thought they were beavers. And some even described them as apes. But the men did not really care what they were. The important thing was that the animals helped save the explorers' lives.

These men were members of an expedition that Russia sent east in the 18th century. Russia was eager to expand, to become larger and stronger. But no one knew what lay beyond Siberia, the easternmost part of the Russian empire. It was known that America existed, but no one knew how far north the continent extended. Approaches to America by European explorers had been westward across the Atlantic Ocean.

Russians and others thought that a great land mass—some called it Gamaland—existed someplace out in the cold sea and dense fogs east of Siberia. The Russians hoped to find and claim this land.

The first expedition east was led in 1730 by Vitus Bering, a native of Denmark who was a captain in the Russian navy. Bering and his men had to march 5,000 miles across Russia and Siberia and build their ships on the Siberian coast. During his first voyage, Bering sailed northwest through what are now known as the Bering Sea and the Bering Strait. (See map on rear endpaper.) He did not sight America and did not find Gamaland, but he did learn that there was no land connection between Asia and America.

Eleven years later Bering was ready to try again. On June 4, 1741, he sailed east from the Kamchatka Peninsula. On July 16 he sighted a towering, snow-clad mountain—now known as Mount Saint Elias, on the coast of Alaska. Bering explored the shore briefly. Then he turned westward, following the chain of volcanic islands we know as the Aleutians. Now he ran into trouble.

His ship, the *St. Peter,* had been poorly built and began to come apart. Supplies of fresh water and food gave out. Crewmen were dying of scurvy, a disease caused by lack of fresh fruits and vegetables. Bering

Adak Island in the cold, bleak Aleutians, sighted by Bering.

himself was seriously ill. The waters of the North Pacific are among the roughest in the world, and the weather during Bering's voyage was stormy. Snow fell and sleet froze on the tattered sails. The ship leaked badly. On a night in November the ship was wrecked

on one of a group of islands. These islands were later named the Komandorski, or Commander, Islands in memory of Commander Bering.

Bering was so ill that he had to be carried ashore, and he died soon afterward. Surviving crew members took shelter in fox dens. The arctic blue foxes were bold and unafraid of human beings. They attacked the intruders, many of whom were too weak to defend themselves. All of the men were miserable, suffering from starvation and the cold.

There were only two good things about the island. One was the sea cow, a kind of manatee. Sea cows could sometimes be found near the shore, where they came to graze on underwater plants. They were huge and fat, awkward and slow-moving, and they could be killed easily. Their meat tasted like beef and was nourishing. There were never very many of these big sea animals, and this particular kind is now extinct.

The other good thing on the island was the sea otter.

The men of the *St. Peter* had seen sea otters as they sailed west along the Aleutian chain. There were many in the sea and some on the shores of the bleak islands.

One of the men on Bering's expedition was a German doctor named Georg Wilhelm Steller. Steller was a close observer of nature. Like others on the expedition, he was not sure what the otter was. He wrote in his journal:

"It was five feet long. The head was like a dog's. . . . There was on both lips a sort of beard. . . . It was full of frolic and played a thousand monkey tricks. Sometimes swimming on one side of the ship, sometimes on the other, looking at it with great amazement. It would come so near the ship that it could be touched with a pole. . . . It often raised one-third of its body out of the water

Playful otters of the North Pacific (from a drawing made in 1906).

and stood erect for a considerable time. It then
suddenly darted under the ship and reappeared
in the same attitude on the other side. It would
repeat this maneuver thirty times together. It
would frequently bring up a sea-plant, not unlike
a bottle gourd. This it would toss about and
catch again in its mouth, playing numberless
fantastic tricks with it."

Marooned on the island after the shipwreck, Steller
and the other men saw many more sea otters. The
otters seemed unafraid of people. It was easy to
approach the animals and kill them with clubs.
The flesh, although strong-smelling and strong-tasting,
could be eaten, and some thought the meat of young
otters was quite good. Better yet, the thick fur could
be made into warm clothing and blankets to protect
the miserable men from the biting cold.

Steller killed many otters himself. And he discovered something else about these unusual creatures.
This was the love of the mothers for their young. In
his journal he told of capturing two young otters:

"The mothers followed me at a distance, like
dogs, calling to their young with a voice like the
wailing of an infant; and when the young ones

heard their mother's voice, they wailed too. I sat down in the snow, and the mothers came close up and stood ready to take the young ones from my hand if I should set them down. . . . After eight days I returned to the same place and found one of the females at the spot where I had taken the young, bowed down with deepest sorrow. Thus she lay, and I approached without any sign of flight on her part. Her skin hung loose, and she had grown so thin in that one week that there was nothing left but skin and bones."

When the survivors of the shipwreck had gained some strength, they broke up the wreckage of the *St. Peter* and used the pieces to build a smaller ship, also called the *St. Peter.* After nine months on the lonely island, they launched their new boat and sailed westward toward Kamchatka, which they had left 14 months earlier. They carried with them many bundles of otter skins—between 800 and 900 pelts.

The new boat leaked badly, too. Cannons, guns, supplies, and baggage were thrown overboard so that the little ship would be lighter and would ride higher in the water. Many bundles of otter skins were also thrown away. Other skins were stuffed into the cracks between the ship's planks to stop leaks. At least one

Sea otters resting on shore in the Aleutians. Otters like these saved the lives of Bering's shipwrecked crew.

sailor is said to have disobeyed orders and to have hidden some pelts under his bunk. Thus, a few of the otter skins arrived safely back in Kamchatka with the men.

The survivors from the *St. Peter* did not think their voyage had been a success. They had not found Gamaland and they did not know quite where they had been. They knew only that they were lucky to be alive.

But they had found the sea otters of the Aleutian Islands—a discovery that led to the exploration of a vast part of the earth.

6
The fur trade

In August 1742, when the survivors of the last Bering expedition returned to Kamchatka, they found a ready market for their furs.

In China, more than 2,000 miles southwest of Kamchatka, wealthy Chinese liked to wear warm, luxurious furs. In the early 18th century Chinese merchants bought a few sea otter skins from the Japanese, who had taken them from the small otter herds around Hokkaido Island. From Russian traders, they bought many more skins of the sable, a land animal trapped by hunters in Siberia.

But sable skins began to get scarce. When the Bering survivors returned, the Russian traders eagerly bought up their sea otter pelts. The traders received high prices for them in China, even though the skins

A Chinese man wearing a sea otter coat. Otter pelts were long in great demand in China.

were ragged and dirty. At first the Russians thought they were trading in beaver skins. Only later did they learn that the skins came from sea otters.

The high prices that the pelts brought, plus the knowledge that there were many more of the animals to be found, started a stampede of Russian hunters. In some ways it was like the Alaska gold rush which came a century and a half later.

Boats had to be built for the fur-hunting expeditions. The men building them knew little about ship design or construction. Building materials were scarce. Uneven, rough boards, cut and shaped by hand, were tied together with thongs of seal and sea lion hides to form hulls. Sails were often made of reindeer skins.

The Russians called these boats *shitikas,* which means "stitched together." Few of them were fit for sailing, and the men using them knew little about the sea. They were professional hunters, not sailors. Nevertheless, they set off on the treacherous sea toward the Commander Islands.

One of the first ships managed to find the island on which Bering and his men had been shipwrecked. The otter herds were still there. The ship brought back a load of 1,600 otter pelts and even more skins of arctic foxes and fur seals. In today's money, the cargo was worth $90,000. More and more boats were built and more expeditions were launched.

Many of the fur-hunting ships were never seen again. Some were lost at sea. Some were wrecked on the islands. And many of the professional hunters were killed by the people who lived on some of the islands.

The Russians called these islanders "Aleuts." The word came from a phrase in the native language which the Russians frequently heard. It was *alik uaia*, which meant "What is it?" This was a question the islanders usually asked when they first saw the Russians and their strange boats.

The people of the Aleutian Islands used weapons and tools made of stone, wood, and bone. Their clothing was made of animal and bird skins. Many wore long shirts, called parkas, made of sea otter skins.

The Aleuts hunted sea otters in kayaks—slender, fragile boats made of sealskin stretched over a wood or bone frame. One or two men rode in each kayak, and many kayaks traveled together, skimming swiftly over the rough water.

When an otter was sighted, the kayaks surrounded it in a wide circle. The otter dove and the Aleuts waited for it to return to the surface. Shouting and

74- 5366

waving their spears, they forced the otter to dive again, before it had time to draw a deep breath. The otter came up more quickly the next time, and again it was forced to dive. Each dive was shorter, until finally the otter was exhausted. It was then killed with spears or clubs.

Aleuts hunting sea otters in a kayak. The man in front holds a spear while the second man paddles.

Young otters were easily caught. The mother otter usually came to the rescue and then she, too, was killed.

At other times the Aleuts spread nets in the kelp beds or along the rocky shore. The otters became entangled in them. Although they bit fiercely at the strands of the net, trying to free themselves, they soon drowned.

The Russians in their clumsy boats were unable to

pursue the sea otters as swiftly and skillfully as the Aleuts in their kayaks. Instead, they traded trinkets—beads, cloth, and bits of metal—for whatever otter skins the Aleuts had. Sometimes the Russians did not bother to trade anything but seized the skins by force.

When the supplies of otter skins on hand were exhausted, the Russians often forced the Aleuts to work for them, hunting otters. It was little better than slavery. In some cases the Aleuts rebelled, although they were peaceful by nature. Both Russians and Aleuts died in fierce battles on the cold and lonely beaches.

Once the otter pelts were collected, they were tied into bundles and taken on a journey of thousands of miles. From the Aleutian Islands they were carried in leaky boats to the Kamchatka Peninsula. From Kamchatka the skins were shipped again, this time 600 miles across the stormy Sea of Okhotsk. Then, by pack horses in summer and dog sleds in winter, they were carried over the plains and mountains of Siberia. Finally they reached the trading center of K'achta on the border of Mongolia.

Here the skins were bartered or sold to Chinese traders. These traders took them on another long journey, often by camel caravan, to the Chinese capital at Peking. An otter skin for which a Russian hunter had paid no more than a few glass beads—if he had paid anything at all—would bring $50 or more in Peking.

The "river of fur" made up of live otters in the Pacific Ocean was now becoming a river of gold flowing deep into the continent of Asia.

An aerial view of a sea otter raft. Such large herds of otters throughout the Aleutians made up the "river of fur."

7
The northwestern frontier

Animal skins have played an important part in shaping the world as we know it today. Much of our own American West first became known to white men because they went there looking for beaver skins. The search for sea otter skins led to the exploration and development of an even larger part of the modern world.

Russian hunters moved farther and farther east through the 700 islands that make up the 900-mile-long Aleutian chain. Hunting camps and supply bases were set up first on the islands, then on mainland Alaska, and finally, much later, as far south as northern California.

The Russians did not tell outsiders about their hunting grounds. The vast triangle between San Francisco, Japan, and the North Pole remained a

An old Russian blockhouse at Sitka, Alaska. This sturdy building gave the Russians a defense against attack.

region of mystery for the rest of the world.

Few Europeans lived in North America at this time. The British colonies that would soon form the United States were little more than a string of settlements along the Atlantic coast. Spain, which controlled Mexico, claimed all of the Pacific coast of North America but had only a few mission settlements—none of them north of San Francisco Bay.

But the Northwest did not remain unknown for long. By the end of the 18th century, British, American, French, and Spanish explorers had found their way into this part of the world.

In 1776—35 years after Bering began his final expedition—another great voyage of discovery began. Captain James Cook, the famous English navigator, left England on the last of his many expeditions. He rounded Africa and sailed through the Indian Ocean and into the Pacific. After reaching the Hawaiian Islands—the first European to do so—he headed for the west coast of North America.

The British Parliament had offered a reward of about $100,000 for the first ship to find a "Northwest Passage"—a sea route across the top of the North American continent. Such a route, if there was one, would make it easier for England to trade with China. Cook hoped to win the prize.

Two years after leaving home, Cook's ships touched the Pacific coast of North America at several points. They then went west along the Aleutian chain and north through the Bering Sea until they were stopped by great masses of sea ice. They returned to the Hawaiian Islands for the winter. There Cook was killed in a misunderstanding with the Hawaiians. But his ships and men made another trip the following year. Once more they cruised north—until they were stopped by the arctic ice—without finding the hoped-for Northwest Passage.

But, like the Russians before them, they found out about sea otters. The Indians of the northwest coast had many sea otter skins, which they willingly traded for brass buttons, fish hooks, nails, and other bits of iron. Cook's men got many pelts from them, particularly around what is now Vancouver Island. But the British sailors, like Bering's men, did not at first realize the value of the skins. They used them casually for warm clothing, rugs, and bed covers.

Later, in Chinese ports, Cook's crewmen found that Chinese merchants eagerly paid gold for otter skins, even though the skins were in poor condition.

News of the wealth to be made from otter skins got back to England and to the newly independent United States. New ships were fitted out and trading voyages

A member of Captain Cook's last expedition sketched this sea otter along the northwest coast.

were begun. Some traders sailed around the tip of Africa, as Cook had done. Others went around Cape Horn, the tip of South America. All headed for the northwest Pacific coast. There they traded their barter goods—iron tools, beads, and cloth—for otter skins. Then they sailed for China to trade the furs for Chinese products—silks, spices, tea, porcelain, ivory, and jade. Finally they returned to London or Boston, where these Chinese goods were in demand.

The Spanish, with their few settlements along the Pacific coast, had known about the sea otters for some time. In 1732 Father Sigismundo Taraval, a Jesuit missionary, had seen many animals in the sea off the coast of Baja California. Although he believed they were beavers, they were almost certainly sea otters.

Somewhat later the Spanish found otters in San Francisco Bay so numerous that they could easily be killed with boat oars. There were thousands more along the coast south of Monterey, the original capital of upper California, and around the islands along the California coast.

The Spanish paid little attention to the otters at first. The meat was not very good to eat—they had plenty of cattle anyway—and fur was seldom used for clothing in a warm climate. But when the Spanish discovered how valuable otter skins were in Chinese markets, they too got into the fur trade. The skins could be traded for Chinese quicksilver (mercury), which the Spanish needed for refining precious metal ores from their Mexican mines.

But the trade in sea otter skins also caused trouble for Spain. The Spanish tried to keep foreign ships of otter hunters and fur traders away from the northwest coast. In 1789 Spain and England almost went to war because Spain had seized some ships in Nootka Sound, near Vancouver Island. Finally, in order to avoid war, Spain gave up trying to control her territory north of California.

Later, when California was under independent Mexican control, more and more Americans came into the area. First there were fur hunters, many of them looking for sea otter skins. There were also whalers,

An otter-hunting and fur-trading settlement on Nootka Sound as it appeared in 1792, soon after Spain and England's dispute over the northwest coast.

Starting in the late 1700s, the Indians of the northwest coast supplied sea otter pelts to fur traders. This Nootka Indian was photographed on an otter hunt in 1915.

adventurers, frontiersmen, and finally settlers. The United States was eager to acquire California and finally did so in 1848 after war with Mexico.

Discoveries made in pursuit of the sea otter helped fix the boundaries of the modern world—and great fortunes were made in the process. The shy sea otter, the innocent cause of so much strife and greed, paid a very high price. It was almost destroyed as a species.

8
The disappearance

Some creatures, like the ancient dinosaurs, have died out and disappeared from the earth from natural causes. But, in the last few thousand years, many have become extinct because of man's carelessness or greed.

Vast herds of buffalo once roamed the western plains of the United States. The Indians who lived there killed some of the animals with arrows and spears for their meat and hides. But there were plenty of buffalo until white men arrived on the plains and killed greater and greater numbers with their rifles. Sometimes they killed for meat, sometimes for hides, and sometimes just for "sport." The buffalo that had once numbered in the millions almost disappeared.

Passenger pigeons were even more numerous than buffalo—so numerous that their flights once darkened the sky. With a single shot a man could kill hundreds of pigeons roosting in a tree—more than anyone could eat. As farming spread, the trees in which the pigeons once mated, nested, and roosted were destroyed to make room for crops. The last passenger pigeon in the world, a bird hatched in captivity, died in a zoo in 1914.

The sea otter faced many of the same dangers as the buffalo and the passenger pigeon. Because the otters stayed together in herds, they were easily killed, particularly with a rifle. Hunters with firearms could kill many more than Indians, Eskimos, and Aleuts had killed with clubs and spears. Hunters could come back to the same herd again and again until all were dead. The value of the otter's fur—for robes and coats and muffs and hats—drove people to slaughter the animals without thought for the future.

A special quality of the otter's fur made more danger for the animal. Most fur-bearing creatures—the fur seal, for example—molt, or shed, their fur at a certain time of year and grow new coats. During the time when they are molting, hunters leave them alone. But the sea otter molts slowly throughout the year, and its fur is always in good condition. As a result, sea otters were hunted and killed the year round.

If the hunters had killed only grown male otters,

the damage might not have been so great. But they took all they could find. The skins of young otters were of little value. But by killing the otter pups, the hunters could lure the mother otters within killing distance.

No one knows how many sea otters existed before hunters began to kill them off. In all the herds from Mexico to northern Japan, there were probably never more than 150,000 otters at any one time—a much smaller population than that of the buffalo or the passenger pigeon.

In the century and a half after Bering's men found the sea otter herds around the Commander Islands, at least half a million otters were killed, and probably many more. The killing went on faster than the otters could breed and bear young to continue the species. Alexander Baranov, a Russian fur trader, collected at least 200,000 otter skins in Alaska and the Aleutians between 1790 and 1817. One of his ships, sailing from Alaska to Siberia, carried a cargo of 15,000 pelts.

But the recorded number of otter skins that reached world markets does not show how many of the animals were actually killed. Many dead otters were never skinned because the hunters could not find their bodies. And ships carrying otter pelts were often lost at sea.

A schooner of an otter-hunting expedition along the northwest coast. Trailing behind it is a small boat used for pursuing and killing the otters once they have been sighted.

Sea otter hunting in the Northwest in the 1800s

A hunter, armed with a rifle, tries to shoot an otter that has come up for air between escape dives.

Otter pelts being stretched and dried, skin side out, on racks aboard a hunting schooner. A live otter pup lies on the deck.

Otter skins, dried and cured, are hung up for airing before being taken to market.

By the middle of the 19th century, sea otters were becoming hard to find. This was one of the reasons Russia lost interest in Alaska and sold it to the United States in 1867. American hunters came into the new territory with high-powered rifles to kill the few otters that could still be found.

A sea otter killed by hunters in the ocean off the Washington coast and brought ashore.

Other fur-bearing animals were becoming scarce, too. One of the most prized was the fur seal. Fur seal skins had never been as valuable as otter pelts, but they were much more plentiful. By the end of the 19th century, fur seals were almost impossible to find.

Finally, in 1911, the United States, Russia, Japan, and Great Britain agreed to stop hunting and killing fur seals. Otherwise the animals would almost surely become extinct. Sea otters were covered by the same agreement. But it really did not matter very much. There seemed to be no otters left to protect.

In 1925 the United States made the Aleutian Islands a wildlife refuge, a place where birds and animals could live safe from hunters. A survey was made to see what kinds of wildlife were in the refuge.

Not a single sea otter could be found.

9
The return

It seemed that man, in his greed and wastefulness, had wiped out another whole species. So far as anyone knew, the sea otter would never be seen again.

But somehow, in secret places undisturbed by man, a few sea otters had managed to escape death and to go on raising pups. Many sea otters prefer cold places, where fewer people live. Almost all sea otters seem to enjoy stormy seas and rocky coasts, both of which are dangerous for boats. There were many places in the Aleutian Islands where people and ships almost never went.

In 1931, six years after the survey in the Aleutians in which no otters could be found, a naturalist visited Amchitka Island. An Aleut asked him if he would like to see something unusual. The naturalist said that he would.

Before dawn the next morning the two men started out. They trudged across the cold, barren island to a place where they had a good view of the ocean. Crouching behind a rock, they watched a kelp bed off-shore. Finally they spotted what they had come to see. There in the kelp bed was a mother sea otter with her pup clutched to her chest. She played with the pup and caressed it lovingly in the way the naturalist had heard about but had never seen.

More otters were seen around Amchitka by sailors in the U.S. Coast Guard in 1935. Still later, during World War II, American fliers were based on Amchitka. They came to know and love the small herds of otters that could be seen around the island—the only cheerful note on the bleak military base.

The otters were coming back in other places, too.

In the old days large otter herds had lived along the central California coast. But the last otter seen there had been killed in 1913. Old people spoke fondly of the sea otters as one of the wonders of times gone by.

South of Monterey lies one of the world's most beautiful coastlines. There are thick forests, lovely coves, and wild, rocky shores. In many places the mountains seem to drop straight into the sea. Back in the hills and valleys live mountain lions, deer, foxes, and coy-

The wild and rocky coast south of Monterey, California.

otes. Along the shore there are thousands of sea birds. And offshore there had once been otters.

Until 1937 few people knew this area. It was very hard to get to. But in that year the state of California completed a highway along the coast, following the valleys, crossing the canyons on high bridges, edging around the steep mountains. Many spots along the highway gave fine views of the ocean, of the surf crashing on the rocks below, and of the great kelp beds offshore. Birds, seals, and sea lions could be seen, and during the winter months gray whales passed by in their annual migration.

Soon after the highway was completed, a southern California husband and wife were admiring the ocean view near San Simeon. In the kelp bed they saw some animals floating on their backs, diving, and eating. They did not know what the creatures were. Driving a little farther, they met a game warden and asked about the animals. The game warden appeared interested—but he did not answer their question. Instead, he jumped in his car and drove off in the direction from which the couple had come. They did not find out for a long time what it was they had seen.

At about the same time another couple also saw some strange animals in the kelp beds at Bixby Creek, near Big Sur. A biologist from Hopkins Marine Station at Pacific Grove identified them as sea otters.

There were at least several hundred otters scattered from Monterey south. Just as in the Aleutians, some otters had survived along the remote California coast. And they had been able to start rebuilding their herds. A few game wardens had known about them, but had kept quiet lest thoughtless people start killing otters again.

Now that the secret was out, the state of California declared the 100 miles of coast south of Monterey a refuge for sea otters. Firearms were outlawed along the coast between the highway and the sea.

Soon the otters became a great tourist attraction. They could easily be seen from the shore—resting in the kelp, diving, eating, playing in the surf, taking care of their pups, and endlessly cleaning and grooming their fur. Some otters even came to live in the boat harbor at Monterey, unafraid of either people or boats. Otter-watching became a popular activity all along the coast, particularly at Pacific Grove, Cypress Point, Point Lobos, Big Sur, and San Simeon.

Today the herds along the California coast have more than 1,000 otters. In the Aleutians there are at least 40,000. Game wardens are trying to control the size of the Aleutian herds, to keep them from getting larger than the supply of food can support. Many otters have been captured and taken to British Colum-

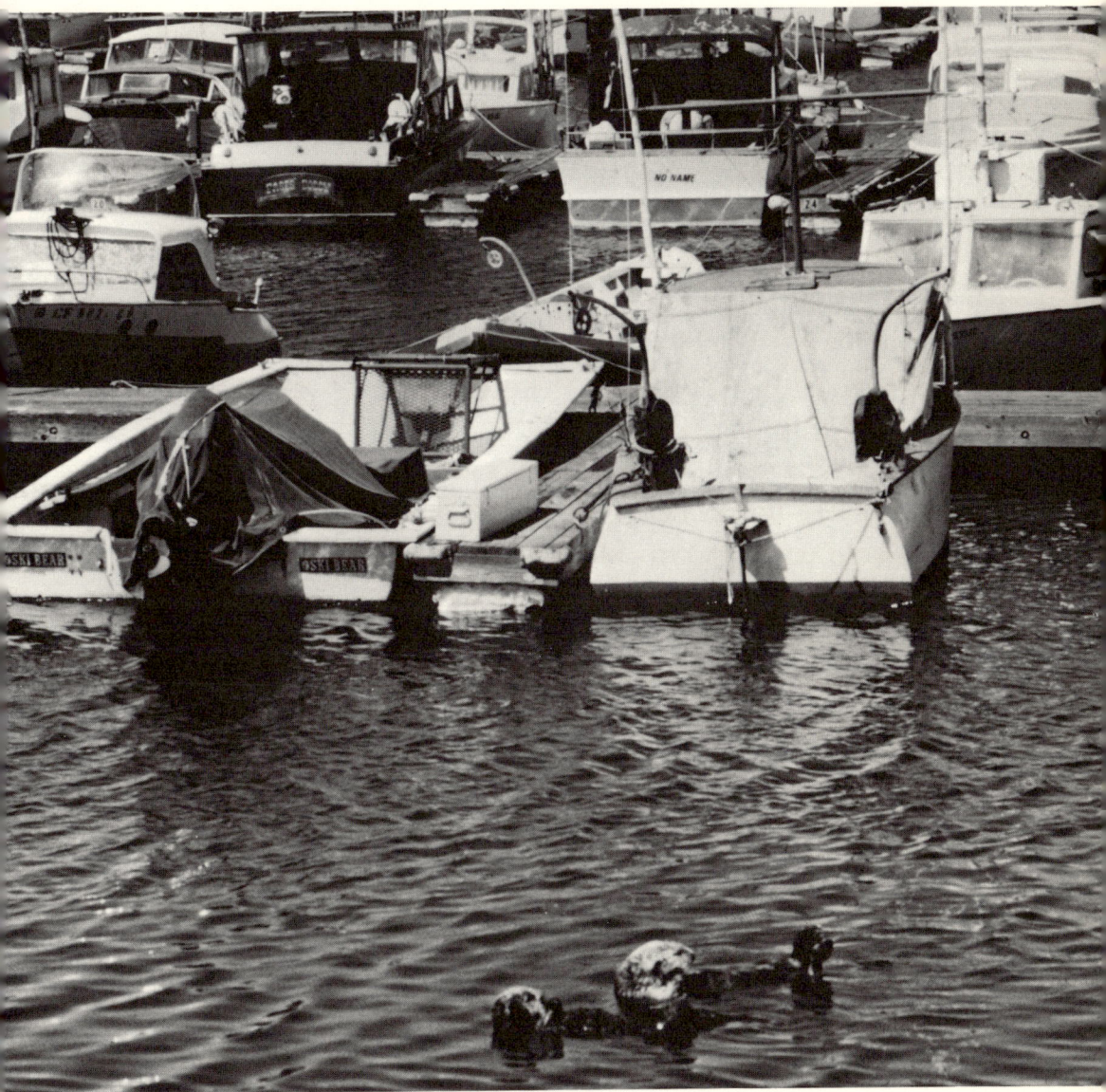

Sea otters floating in the Monterey boat basin.

bia, Washington State, and Oregon, places where great otter herds once lived. With luck, otters may thrive in these places again.

The otters in California and the more numerous ones in the Aleutians are almost identical in appearance. But differences in the sea and in the climate cause some differences in the way they live and behave.

For instance, those in California seldom come ashore unless they are injured, sick, or dying. Those in the north frequently come on shore to rest or sleep during severe storms. In Bristol Bay, northeast of the Aleutians, sea ice occasionally forms, and the otters are sometimes forced to climb out and look for open water where they can dive for food. There have never been very many people in the Aleutians. The otter may feel safer in coming ashore there than in California, where there have always been more people along the coast.

Unlike the California otter, the Aleutian otter gathers food without a stone tool. The creatures it hunts are not attached to the rocks and are not hard to break open, so it does not need a tool. But in captivity the Aleutian otter, if given some hard-shelled clams and a stone, will use the stone to break the clamshells, just as the California otter does.

Some observers believe the California or "southern" sea otter is a distinct subspecies—that is, a different kind of animal within the sea otter family. Whether different or not, the sea otters, both north and south, have come back. And people are no longer allowed to shoot them.

But sea otters are still not free from danger.

Driven out of the water by a bad storm, a northern sea otter walks awkwardly across a stony beach.

10
Otters, urchins, kelp, and man

Sea otters have little to fear from other animals. There have been stories of bald eagles seizing otter pups and flying away with them, but this happens rarely. A few otters seem to have been killed by sharks, but only a few. Killer whales, some of the most savage and hungry creatures of the ocean, show no interest in sea otters. The black-and-white killers will swim past otters to attack seals, sea lions, or other whales. When the killer whales approach, the otters usually stop eating and playing, and they are not harmed.

But the sea otter faces many other dangers—all man-made.

One of the commonest dangers to otters along the California coast is boat propellers. Careless people driving motorboats at high speed fail to see otters in the water ahead and run into them. The propeller blades often cripple or kill the animals.

Another danger is silt—loose earth from farmland and road construction and ashes from burned-over forests. Silt drifts into the ocean, blanketing the bottom and killing marine plants. With these plants gone, the fish and shellfish that depend on them for food and shelter disappear—and these creatures are the otters' food supply.

Oil slicks, always a threat along the California coast, are another danger to otters. Sometimes an offshore oil well begins to leak or a ship carrying a cargo of oil is wrecked. The oil spreads out over the surface of the ocean, making beaches unusable, choking sea life, killing birds. If such an oil slick reached an otter herd, the animals would be doomed. With their fur soaked in oil, the otters could no longer stay warm, dry, and afloat. They would soon die.

The biggest mass killing of sea otters in recent history took place in November 1971. At that time the United States Atomic Energy Commission set off an underground nuclear test explosion at Amchitka Island in the Aleutians, home of one of the largest herds of sea otters. The shock effect of the explosion killed many kinds of wildlife—including about 1,000 otters.

Oil slicks and atomic explosions are, fortunately,

rare. But one of the gravest dangers to otters is always present. This is pollution, a threat to all living creatures. Germs and poisons—some from sewage, some from industrial wastes, some from insect-killing chemicals used in farming—often end up in the ocean. Some scientists say our oceans are dying because of this pollution. They mean that the oceans are becoming unable to support life. If the oceans die, the sea otters will of course die too. Meanwhile biologists are studying the effect on otters of such poisons as mercury and cadmium, both of which are found in water where otters live.

If the otters should disappear again, many people would be saddened. But their disappearance would have a far greater effect than that.

The sea otter is an essential part of the natural community in which it lives. Such communities are called "ecosystems." The animals and plants within an ecosystem depend upon each other and are balanced by each other. When one ecosystem is upset or destroyed, other ecosystems are usually affected as well.

The otter's community is the kelp bed. Kelp is a strange plant. It usually grows where the ocean floor is rocky. Instead of having roots at its base, it has a cluster of branches called "holdfasts" which anchor it to the ocean floor. The holdfasts do not bring food to the rest of the kelp plant as the roots of land plants do.

A wary otter, seen from below. Sensing a threat, the otter has ducked its head underwater to stare at the photographer beneath it. Its forepaws remain above water in the alarm position.

They only keep the kelp from being washed away. Kelp absorbs its food from the sea water. The stronger the ocean currents are, the more food the kelp can absorb. Healthy kelp grows at the rate of a foot or two a day—the fastest-growing plant in the world.

The kelp beds shelter the many fish and shellfish that the sea otter hunts. They are also a rich source of food for man. For thousands of years man has known that fishing is good around kelp beds. In places where the kelp has disappeared, the fishing has become poorer.

Kelp itself has been used for many years as a food supplement for humans and animals and as fertilizer to help produce other foods. More recently kelp has been harvested as a rich source of various chemicals and minerals, which it has soaked up from the ocean and stored. Among them are iodine, vitamins, salts, and potassium.

One of the most valuable substances found in kelp is "algin." A spoonful of algin dissolved in a quart of water makes the water almost as thick as molasses. One of the commonest uses of algin is in ice cream. It prevents the water in ice cream from forming into crystals of ice, and keeps the ice cream smooth. Algin is also used in cake icing, salad dressings, paints, dyes, glues, and many other products.

Kelp-harvesting ships cut off the top part of the plant—the canopy that spreads out over the ocean surface—and take it ashore for processing. This cutting encourages the kelp to grow even faster, and does no lasting harm to the marine life in the kelp bed.

A kelp-harvesting ship. As the ship moves slowly through the kelp bed, it cuts the seaweed three feet below the surface and moves it on board by conveyor belts.

Sea urchins feeding on a small kelp plant. The leaves are already half-eaten.

Two things discourage the growth of kelp. One is warmer water than the plant is used to. But ocean currents warm up only rarely.

The other and much greater danger is the sea urchin. A relative of the starfish and sand dollar, the sea urchin lives on the bottom of the ocean. It is covered with long, needle-sharp spines which can be very painful to step on. Small sea urchins are often found in tide pools. Much larger ones, up to seven inches across, live in deep water. Some are black, some purple, some red, some green.

Sea urchins grow rapidly and lay eggs by the thousands. They feed on kelp, and in doing so they frequently destroy it. Once they have eaten through the stem at the bottom, the rest of the plant drifts away and dies, usually ending up as a smelly mess on the beach.

When kelp is healthy and growing, it forms an underwater garden. But when sea urchins destroy it, the garden becomes a marine desert in which almost nothing lives.

Scientists are studying how to replant kelp beds that have been destroyed by sea urchins. And companies that harvest kelp have hired divers to go down and kill some urchins. This they sometimes do by smashing the creatures with a hammer.

But the sea otter is a much better urchin-killer. Urchins are a favorite food of the otters. With their great appetite and remarkable diving skill, the otters can keep this marine pest under control. In places where the sea otters disappeared early in the 20th century, the sea urchins multiplied. The kelp beds began to disappear, and so did the fish and other marine creatures that lived there.

An otter swims upward with a sea urchin it has just found.

Thus the kelp bed depends on the sea otter as much as the otter depends on the kelp. And man benefits from the whole ecosystem as long as he does not upset it.

Unfortunately, there is yet another threat to the sea otter and its community. This arises from the abalone industry, which finds sea otters a nuisance.

The otters like to eat abalone, too, although they seem to prefer sea urchins. During the otters' long absence, abalone became more abundant along the coast of California and Mexico. This shellfish had long been a food delicacy in the Orient, and it began to be popular in the United States.

Men harvest abalone by prying them from underwater rocks with an iron tool. The fleshy part of the abalone is cut out, pounded until it is tender, then sold as a luxury food. The abalone business is not a large one, but some commercial fishermen depend on it for a living.

When the surviving sea otter herds along the California coast began to recover, the abalone divers complained. Abalone, they said, were becoming scarce because of the otters, and if the abalone disappeared the divers would be out of work.

Game wardens captured some of the otters that had been feeding in the abalone beds and took them to other locations. Some of the otters died during the transfer. Others quickly found their way back to the places from which they had been taken.

A few of the abalone divers took matters into their own hands. They began shooting otters with rifles. In 1970 and 1971, fifty otters that had been killed with rifle bullets were found along the California coast. Some abalone divers were arrested and fined.

It is true that there are fewer abalone than there once were. It is also true that the otter likes to eat them just as humans do. But abalone are becoming scarce all along the Pacific coast, even in places where the otter has not returned. Man's appetite seems to be just as destructive to the abalone as the otter's.

Almost all creatures in a crowded world face some dangers. Although some of them manage to live with their dangers, other creatures have been overcome. They have disappeared and never will be seen again. Some, such as the brown pelican, the bald eagle, and the peregrine falcon, may soon become extinct.

The playful, affectionate sea otters have been to the very edge of extinction. But, being very hardy animals, the otters have come back, to the delight of everyone who sees them in their kelp-bed homes. With a little luck, a little help, and a lot of consideration, they may be around for a long time to come.

A sea otter feasts on an abalone.

Index

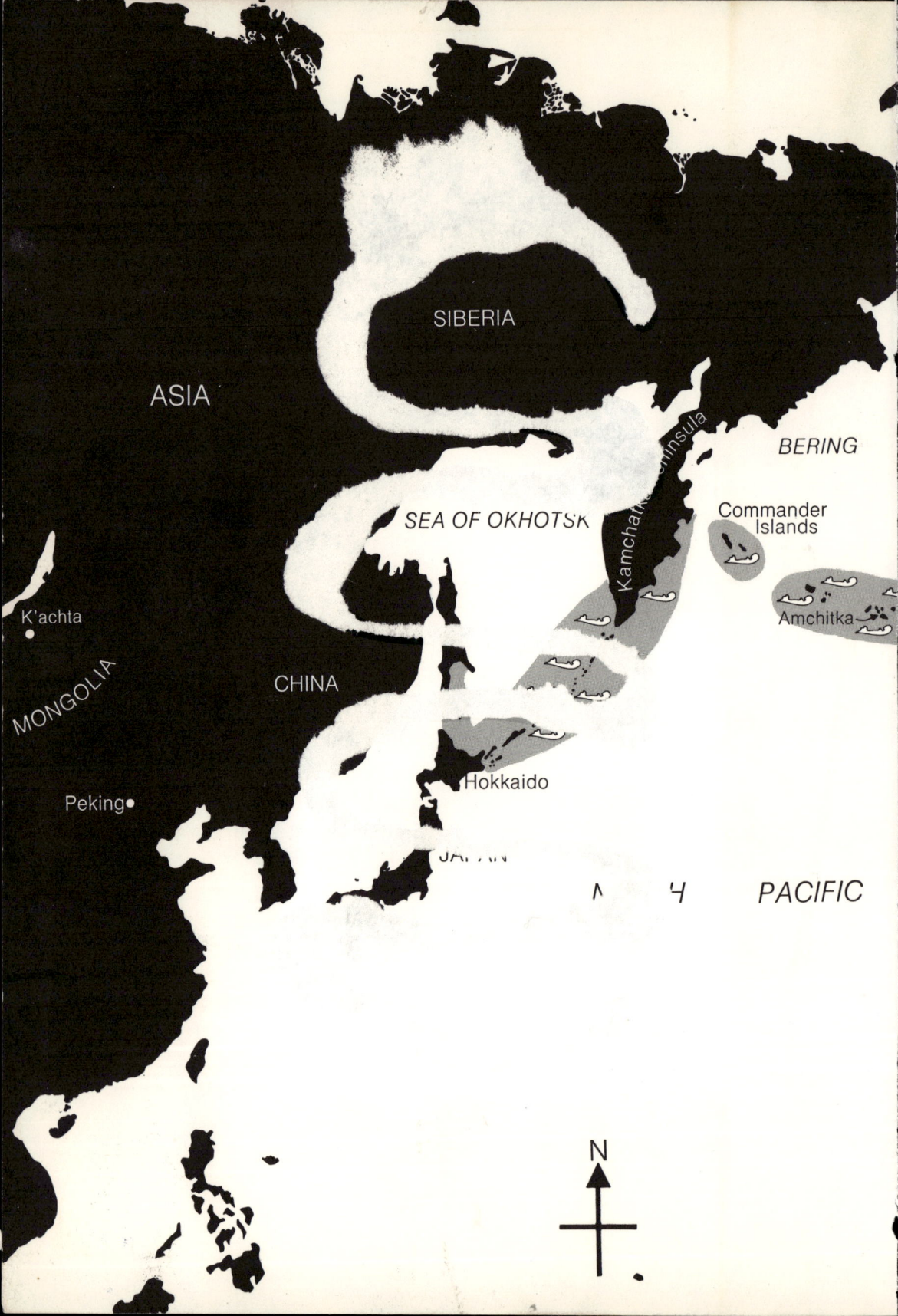

ASIA

SIBERIA

SEA OF OKHOTSK

Kamchatka Peninsula

BERING

Commander
Islands

Amchitka

K'achta

MONGOLIA

CHINA

Hokkaido

Peking

JAPAN

PACIFIC

N